Cover: Marta Moran Bishop

Art: Marta Moran Bishop

Printed in the United States of America

Crowe Press LLC

WWW.CROWEPRESS.COM

WHEN I WAS NOT MYSELF

This book is dedicated to all those who have faced trial, error, loss and continue to survive even through what may appear to be insurmountable odds. To those whose spirit of life keeps hope and love alive.

Although the poetry in this book is primarily by Marta Moran Bishop, we are thankful that Helen Diessner and Roman Nyle allowed us to include one of their poems.

When I Was Not Myself

Marta Moran Bishop

with

Helen Diessner
&
Roman Nyle

Contents

Contents

Contents

Contents

WHEN I WAS NOT MYSELF

There is beauty in my soul
And kindness in my heart
A sadness for mistakes I made

When I was not myself

It's easy to go astray
And lose oneself
When you follow not your spirit
Or the whispers in your head

The desire not to hurt
Or disappoint can overwhelm
The pressure to fit in
The need to belong
Can blind you, so you cannot see

When you are not yourself

I do not seek to judge
Those I once called friend
For I know not their pain
Or what is in their hearts
Nor could I have sought the answers

When I was not myself

I honor all the memories
Of those that I have lost
For even in my anguish
I learned a lot.

To listen to the whispers
The screaming of my spirit
Even when it sees those things I wish weren't so
I am grateful to those who stayed
When I was in the dark

It can't have been easy
But you helped me find my way
As I walk toward the light
And listen to my soul
As it takes the splendor in

And I become myself

I'll remember those days of dark despair
When the world closed in
A few scars will remain upon my heart
From lessons I have learned

When I was not myself

I'll not judge myself
For those mistakes I made
Nor flog my spirit bloody
But take them as lessons learned
For you cannot go back

As I travel on my path
Through the deep dark woods
Muddy black bogs of loss
As I make my way back
Into the beauty that I am

The darkness and despair
The loneliness and sorrow
Will be a memory of the days

When I was not myself

WHERE DID YOU GO

That joyful girl
With life and love ahead
I thought I'd conquer the world
And dance upon a rainbow
Hold stars in my hands
Hair drifting in the breeze

Have the years caught up
Life's lessons too hard
To find solace in the trees
At water's edge rebirth
The suns light shining on me
Quiet all around

Except for the sounds of nature
Birds singing and chattering
Water skipping over the rocks
Skimming the shore
My furred and feathered friends
Save me, give comfort in my need

Unseen and unknown
But for a few, who fear to care
Treasure my solitude
When it is my choice
Not forced upon me
In the solitary confinement

That once became my life
It is in that quarantine I forget
How to laugh or smile
In the cell I'm confined to
By those who wish me gone
Who'd rather I was a robot
Not a human being

NO TIME

No time to sort through
The trauma and sorrow
When life moves to fast
With blow after blow
As it comes from all sides

No time to sort through
To find your place
Time is not on your side
So much on your plate
Too many changes

It makes life hard
Leaving you reeling
When faced with the truth
Too much has happened
Life has changed too quickly

From having a home
To homeless you go
Working and working
To no work at all
Surgery, more surgery

What you once knew is lost
Finding yourself
Among the shadows and dust
Of what once was

And what is now true
I'll pick up the pieces

Sort through the mess
Put life back together
Stronger and better
Fearless I go
Live in the present
Into the future I go
As I sort through the past
Let go of what I must
Embrace the new me
With love and patience for self

SING ME A LULLABY

Just when I think I understand
Clearly at last
Another blow is right in front of me
Almost too much to bear
Please, sing me a lullaby
Let me rest my head upon your shoulder

Whisper to me of love
Bright flowers and singing birds
Animals at play
Moonlit nights to guide my way
Days of joy and laughter
Please, sing me a lullaby

One that promises, things will be alright
Happiness will return
Without fear of tomorrow
A place to watch the sun
Glinting through the leaves
Please, sing me a lullaby

Tell me of days to come
Where water bounces over rocks
Cool soft breezes touch my skin
Bees humming, butterflies skimming
Please sing me a lullaby
Let me rest my head upon your shoulder

SECOND PLACE

All my life I've lived
Putting myself second place
Everyone's needs before me
Who was to blame
Why me of course.

MISUNDERSTANDING

If it's something I did
I don't know what
The message was clear
It's been for a while
It makes me unsure
Of just what to say
And why it is that we lost so much

What was the trigger
That made things all change
Am I misreading
That could be the case
Too much has happened
In too short of time
I am still reeling

I'm going to take time
To sort through some things
To get my life straight
To pull it together
The strings of my past
And let go of what's needed
No wish to repeat

This path I've been on
Of sadness and pain
And misread signals
So please understand
I can't be here right now

Perhaps just for a while
Maybe a bit longer
I care just the same
It's not about you.

CHOICES

Have you ever tried to see
From another's point of view
Attempted to walk in their shoes for a bit

For just one brief moment
Let go of your ego
Look past your own nose

Gaze anew at the world
Eyes unclouded by shared past
The perception of what was

Do you believe things untainted
Past baggage not valid
We can look beyond
But only together

Please. see me as I am
And no longer allow others
To paint you false pictures

So, you can believe
Untruths that suit your agenda
At the expense of all others

MEMORIES

For a moment time stood still
As I looked upon the photographs
She took that last year
We lived together

The day we buried, Poofie
The day we brought Peter home
That big orange cat
So happy to have a family

He looked at the tree
So brightly lit
Cat toys strewn
All around the floor
And new friends to love

Peter was so dear
To our departed Poofie
He saw his poor body
Laying upon a white cloth
Soon to be burial clothes

A favorite toy tucked next to him
Peter stood, sniffed and looked
Then from amongst the Christmas toys
He found one he liked
In his mouth, he carried it
And laid it upon the white cloth

A gift to the cat
We loved so dearly
Whose death we mourned
Peter recognized the gift
Poofie had given him
And gave honor back

He wasn't a replacement
But, if Poofie had lived
Peter mightn't have a home
Both hold a place
In our hearts and souls
For none are replaceable
Each one their own

But we wouldn't have been looking
And Peter would not have a home
He sat in the window for an hour that day
Upon the perch where Poofie once sat
And watched me bury
Our old friend

It's been sixteen plus years
Since those pictures were taken
And nearly fourteen since I found
Those rolls of film
Among my mother's things
After her death

I kept putting them in a safe place
And finding them now and then
Today, I picked them up
No longer a roll of film
But precious memories
Of those I loved and lost

LOST IN ASPERGER'S?

Sometimes it seems no matter what I do
No matter what I feel or how much I care
I am fated to walk through this life alone
Lost friends, lost family, closeness gone
Doomed to become casual acquaintances

Now and forever walking on eggshells
Always careful of how much I show
How much of me will you accept my friends
What happens when we meet, will it change it all
Thenceforth it seems I am out in the cold

I wish I knew what I was doing wrong
Maybe, I am not supportive enough
Perchance, I have stepped to close to your space
Or maybe, it's just my own awkwardness
Never knowing what it is that is expected of me

HELP NOT HINDER

I'd like to take the pain away
Make all the hurt and sorrow go
Bring a bit of joy to you
Shine light in dark places too
All I have is my heart to give

And a shoulder if you need it
I pray I help and not hinder
Bring a smile to your face
Alas, I can only love you
And try not to add to your woes

NOT A SOCIAL BUTTERFLY

I'm not a social butterfly
Though it probably seems that way
I am not good in groups you see
Always, feeling awkward

Afraid if you see all of me
You'll think me a foolish clown
I am just like everyone
I want to like and be liked back

We all wish for understanding
We all wish for approval too
Have people care for us
Be accepted for who we are

Much has happened these last few years
To cause me pause and wonder
What I have done so awfully wrong
Or if I'm just a nut

I've always been shy you see
So, when I feel my lowest
I focus on the one before me
For I've no idea where I stand

MISREADING

Sometimes I misread things
At times I misunderstand
But. I'll never intentionally
Seek to hurt you

I am only human

Forgive me my blunders
And the mistakes that I will make
I'm not always right you know
Nor am I always wrong.

I am only human

A YEAR IN SIX DAYS

What happened the year
I was eleven
I don't remember
Six days of that year
Hold all memory I fear

Sometimes things trigger
Darkness and panic
But nothing that is concrete
It must have been bad
What happened that year?

I should remember
How could I forget
Why do I panic
When smells remind me
Of what I don't know

Five of us children
Have no memory
Of that whole year
How can that happen
A year in six days

LOST

When we were little
You were my sunlight
In darkness you glowed
In daylight we laughed

Ages it lasted
Our hearts connected
And lives intertwined
One day it was gone

Your anger replaced
The happiness was gone
For what I don't know
Your vision is marred

It seems you expect
Me to be someone else
I really don't know who
For I haven't changed a lot

I've grown a bit too
And opened my eyes
Refused to be used
Stuck up for myself

Goodbye to the hurt
I can't live for you
And be a doormat
For you to walk on.

FINDING MYSELF

Once I had a hug club
Exclusive as could be
Not by gender or race
Nor nationality
Religion didn't matter
What's in your hearts the key

That day has come and gone
To my sorrow and regret
No longer do I work
In a place of hugs and fun
I'll find my hugs in smiles
In my love of life
Furred and Feathered friends
The beauty of the forest
The power of the wind
Swirling of a brook
The Ocean pounding on the shore.

IS IT DEATH WE FEAR

Is it death we fear
Or living that we're afraid of
To ride the wind across the sky

Sail our ship through rough waters
Breezes blowing through our hair
Sand between our toes

A horse's mane whipping in our face
Legs wrapped around and arms out wide
Laughing, singing, feeling, living

A WORK IN PROGRESS

There are things I didn't learn
Growing up as I did
Always moving so much
Never settling down

Lasting friendships were rare
I didn't stay long enough
Transient lifestyles
Serve to make one unsure

Of many things it seems
Those who've known me for years
And understand me well
Forgive me my blunders

When it's not understood
I retreat when sorting
Through things in my head
Talk things out with a few

I'm a work in progress
And will get it one day
So, until that day comes
Please forgive me, my foibles.

HOW EASY IT IS

How easy it is to fool oneself
When you love the people involved

When our hearts tied to memories
Of times and places long gone

How easy it is to fool oneself
When you love the people involved

Years of heartache have come and gone
Your head still buried in sand

How easy it is to fool oneself
When you love the people involved

After the tide has come and gone
And your head no longer buried

How easy it'd be to fool yourself
Because of the love you still feel

Seeing clearly has its rewards
To look on the beauty of life

Some days the heartache makes you weep
For the loss of the fool you were

It's so easy to fool yourself
When your heart longs for yesterday

Yet the growth of soul opened wide
The future to make all your own

How easy it would be to fool yourself
Because of the love you still feel

SHINING LIGHT BEFORE DESPAIR

Atop a hill. a citadel stood
For a brief. moment in time
It gleamed a light of hope
A shining ray upon the hill
The chance of freedom from despair

Its rooms were filled with grace. dignity and laughter
Inside its walls intelligence lived. wit and honor too
History will mark these years
Agonize over what came after
When faith was lost in the land

When the suffering of many grew
That came from the choices of the few
And the apathy of the others
Who helped usher in what was to come
A world of demigods and destruction

Lost was clean air and water
The rivers carried the dead
The poor. elderly and young suffered
By the hands of the God of Greed
All mourned the loss of what was

Before hate and fear
Reigned the land
And darkness filled the earth
But. history will remember
The shining light upon the hill

Before destruction came
When the world still had a chance
When peace was a possibility
If. fear and hate were beaten back
And the demigods had not won

I mourn the loss already
Before it is completely gone
My heart still hopes
Because we fight
For freedom. love
And the light upon the hill

TRANQUILITY

I feel your presence in the breeze
As it brushes across my skin
Lifting my hair with its gentle caress
Comforting me in its embrace

I see you in the trees
All aglow in mornings light
And the beauty of the leaves
In the starkness of a winters night

I smell your essence in Mother Earth
The scent of new blossoms in the spring
And the green moss upon the earth
That springs beneath my feet

You warm me with your fire
On a cold winters night
And in the brightness of the stars
I see your light

You lift me with the violence
Of the storm sweeping across the heavens
Cleansing me with the rain
Leaving me at peace in its wake

In the heat of the summer
The water cools me off
Softly rolling in moonlight
Gliding over golden sand

Your spirit clings to me
As it sinks deep into my soul
Ever so slightly changing me
With your gentle melody.

MY EDGAR

Though winter is upon us
The days cold and dreary
My heart and soul burn with undying fire
Though our time was merely a glance

One stolen moment, long ago
That keeps the embers burning
Lights my spirit from within
Searing and haunting me still

The neighbors think me odd
Though kindly take my charity
At night I walk the floors
Till' Lavinia knocks upon the door

Anon, Anon I say to her
Not even to my dear sister, can I speak your name
Nor say what is in my heart that keeps me up at night
Perhaps tomorrow for a moment, I'll quench it

And lay upon the cold, white snow
Make an angel in the snow
For you my dearest Edgar
The one that makes the fire burn within my soul

Yours Emily

DARLING EMILY

Do not fear my darling girl
Nevermore was not meant for you

I lost my wife of latter-day
Neither friend or foe can council me

Nor can I find solace in a bottle
With temperance still in toe

For did I not promise upon my soul
To give up drink and all its woe

Instead I took pen and paper
To drown my sorrow upon

None can say I was a faithful husband
My heart lay elsewhere

Still I loved in my own way
She who now lies dead

Who was the Angel of my younger days
Before I grew and drunk my way
From bed to bed to bed

I did not do right by her
And now cannot amend

Those broken promises once I made
That time has come and gone

But for you my Emily
The bride who should have been

I hold only love within my heart
Neither temperance or grief can sway

Our bond of mind and soul
Never fear my Emily, nevermore is not for you

It is only the grief and guilt I feel
For the loss of one who held me dear
Once upon a time.

Edgar

LOST, ALL LOST

Why are you sitting there old mother?
In that wheelchair on the street.
Clinging to your little dog and crying.
Are you sick or just lost?
Where is your family?
Where is your home?

Lost, all lost.
First, they took away my Medicare
And I couldn't get my medication
Then they took my social security
And I couldn't pay my bills
Finally, it was my home they took.
And now I'm on the street.

What happened to your savings?
That little pension that helped you live
There must be a place for you to go.
Where is your family old mother?
Why don't you live with them?
You can't just sit here, you'll die you know.

Lost, all lost.
My daughter has her children.
They are struggling just to live.
Her husband lost his job.
And cannot find another
Their savings are all gone.

There is no place for me.

My son's wife doesn't want me
She said I'd be a bother
I should go into a home
Where there are nurses to look after me.
She doesn't understand.
Those homes want money too.

Lost, all lost.
They said I should have saved more.
I thought I had enough
With my little pension
Social security and Medicare
Which my husband and I paid into
For the fifty years we worked.

Old mother, you can't stay here
Sitting in the street
There must be somewhere you can go
Someone who'll take you in.
Perhaps your church can help
And find you a place to live?

Lost, all lost.
My church is overpacked
With all those who came before me.
The ones who started with less.

And lost their homes
When Medicare and social security were cut.
Thank you for your concern.
I see you have problems too.
Did you lose your job?
Or was your pay cut in half?
Are your savings all depleted?
When minimum wage was cut.

Alas, old mother, you are right.
My children can no longer go to school
Since, they privatized everything
They have no future that I can see
Unless, they live long enough
And go fight in one of the wars.

Lost, all lost.
Perhaps, young man
You can get a job, burying the dead
Who died before their time.
The soldiers, hurt in the wars
The old without a home
And the babies to be born.

All gone, lost, all lost.

THE SAILOR

Upon the deck he stands, gray gone from his head
Hair blonde again, covered by a sailor's cap

Far off in the distance his blue eyes stare
Long gone the haunted look from his countenance
Forever forward he sails, to new shores he goes

Wind whips through strands of hair uncovered by his hat
All smiles and hope are his once more
Life begins anew for him
Still he loves those his mortal body left behind

Forever, watching over, holding tight those he loves
Who will one day start afresh with him, in a new land
beyond these shores

RENEWAL

I love the forest with its dark shady paths
Sunlight filtering down through branches and leaves
Squirrels and chipmunks scampering all around
Quiet and peaceful away from the noise
Of mankind's chatter, hammers and horns

Nature around me abounding with life
Listening to sounds of the birds and crickets
The play of water rushing over rocks
Glimmering sunlight catching whitecaps

A fox peeking at me through leaves and brush
Off in the distance a shy little deer
With a majestic buck, wings on its feet
Owl hooting the last goodbye as dawn breaks

All of nature's beauty quiets my thoughts
Seeps deep into my heart
Filling it with a natural peace
Mysterious glory seeking my soul
Making me one with trees and sunlight

As I walk along this dark, shady path
I am filled with the sounds of love
The essence of life is in these woods
If you walk quietly and allow it in
You too can be filled with its brimming light

SOMETHING ABOUT THE WATER

Something about the water
Jumping and playing over rocks
As it swiftly moves down toward
The beaver's dam and stops
Frothing, foaming as it hits
A joyful melody

Something about the water
That makes you want to smile
Sit and sing a soothing song
And watch the sunlight play
Upon the waves
As they dance across the sandy beach

Something about the water
As it brings peace to your soul
Fills you with the power
Of the storm within your soul
And peace in your heart
With the beauty in its many forms.

SMILIE

There once was a girl nicknamed Smilie
Whose family all called her Kiley
The grin on her face from ear to ear
Gave all who saw her leave with good cheer
Not one could keep a frown on their face
Instead joy filled their hearts for a space

Deep in her soul lights danced through her eyes
Her heart full of laughter and never sighs
For friend or stranger, she shared her smiles
Glorious grin that went on for miles
Heartaches were hers, but the joy to deep
Somehow smiles from her spirit did leap

Despite hurt and unhappy times
Days of hunger and mimicking mimes
Or the patched clothes and the hand-me-downs
Deep in her spirit she wore all gowns
Upon her head was a golden crown
For in her heart there wasn't a frown

She felt blessed with love in her heart
Beauty abounded in all her art
Though sometimes the sadness came first
In the end the joyfulness did burst
And the girl whose family named Kiley
Still grinned when she was called Smilie

GLIMMER OF LIGHT

Through the darkness I have walked
Sometimes only a glimmer of light to see my way
To the bright and sunny days to come
When that glorious world I behold will be mine

For even on the dark and gloomy days
A glimpse or a moment. a bit can be found
One can hold on. until that time comes
When you step again through the door
Of beauty and light

Where you walk in harmony
Joyously
Radiantly
Resplendently
With beauty and light

BEAUTY BEYOND

Clouds black and full, fill the sky
With yesterday's poignant memories
Lazily they drift across the heavens
As the sunlight filters through

A rainbow may pop up today
As a further sign from above
That yesterday's rainy day
Can be replaced with fresh delights

To fill our hearts and souls
With the beauty that can be ours
If we can look beyond
And let times gone be forgotten
Then a new day will begin

UPWARD, ONWARD

Through the darkness
The heart rises
And spirit shines
As an eagle
We can soar
Above the clouds
Passing the moon
Flying through the stars
Gliding, wings spread
Ever upward
Always onward

Let go sweet soul
Of all that is past
We cannot change
Mistakes once made
Instead we'll learn
Becoming more
Then once we were
Flying, soaring
Upward, onward

CHROME

Across the field they ran
And through the trees they flew
Up the hill they scampered
Over the river they jumped

Regal is her fur friend
Majestically me moves
Long legs and golden mane
And tail that flows behind

His silver eyelashes
Frame loving brown eyes
Speaking volumes
A lifetime together
Continuously friends
And forever family

LIVE AND LEARN

I lay upon the bed and think
About the days gone by
The mark they left upon me
And the new days yet to come

I glory in the life I've lived
Knowing perfect I am not
More to grow, more to learn
To become fully me

I learned its sometimes necessary
To let another go
And not attempt to reconcile
The misunderstandings from long ago

Those two paths that once had crossed
Had long since gone their separate ways
The chasm much too deep and wide
No longer can it be spanned

Sometimes another doesn't wish
To build that bridge, nor understand
Judgments already made
Remember all the best and wish them well

For the stint is in the past
Now, your time is better spent losing the regrets
This is not the period to say
I wish I had, I wish I hadn't

But, instead look at what part you played
In the destruction of it all
What insecurities did you have?
Where should your boundaries be

Learn and grow
From the loss of the past
And the beauty yet to come
Look forward to each new day
With eyes of joy and sorrow gone

BORN OF TWO WORLDS

Born on the wrong side of the tracks
From her parents she had
A foot in each world
Belonging in neither while growing up
Afraid she wouldn't fit in
Shy and lonely, quietly observing
Born of two worlds
Belonging in neither
Never knowing
Always searching

She felt the star within herself
Feared it was all in her mind
From mother's stories
Of how life had been
And father's drinking bouts
Born of two worlds
Belonging in neither
Never knowing
Always searching

LET YOUR LIGHT SHINE ON

Come out of your shell little girl
Let your true light shine
Don't allow the losses
Or the times you've lost yourself
To lesson who you are
And who you may become

Don't let the past define you
Or the times you weren't yourself
When you didn't know what was expected
And your life was upside down
Of all the times and places
When others put you down

They can only have power
If you allow it to be
Even a year in solitary confinement
Seven years watching your back
Cannot harm you now
Unless you give them sway

Others can judge you
If that is their choice
They know not what it cost
And may think it trivial if they did.
But seven years of fear leaves its mark nonetheless
Though you can survive it

And once again find glory
Pride in what you do
Even in your shyness
And knowing they are judging
Doesn't need to harm you
As long as you let the beauty in.

The beauty that is within
And wisdom you have learned
For even in your shyness
The kindness and love glow forth
You don't need another
To tell you what to be

Nor someone else to define you
Or someone to let you fly
Your life is your own
To make what you want
And glory in the greatness
That is in your heart.

DEATH ISN'T

Death isn't only about the dead and dying
It is also about those who are living
The mother, father, husband, wife
The lover, child, sister, brother
Caretaker, and friend

It is about the pain of watching
Your loved one waste away
And their life's blood drain
Helplessly watching and waiting

And wonder if you have done enough
If you were there for them
If what you gave was sufficient
When your strength was gone

While you watched, hope absent
Your loss already keen upon you
Guilt for things undone
The unsaid hanging over you.

With your life already in shambles
The loneliness lurking in the shadows
Helpless to do more
Hopeless to fight this horrible battle

For the one you love
And the pain you feel

That is both theirs and yours
Consumes you, devours you

Leaving nothing in its wake
To help you carry on
Accept the dregs of your strength
To pull you forward

To the final days
When they are gone
And you are left alone
With only guilt and loss

The hope and prayer that they
Understood the love you felt
And how hard you tried
Each moment, each day.

No death isn't only about
The dead and dying
It is also about the ones
Left behind to suffer the loss

And wonder if you did all you could
For no matter how much, you gave
No matter how much you loved
A part of you is lost when they pass.

Hold on to this at the end
When they are gone
And you are alone
They love you still and understand.

CAUSE AND EFFECT

Mr. Cause and Miss Effect
Tried so hard to be perfect
They were human, so you see
When Cause fell down on his knee
And became a big baby

Effect said to discover
It's your fault not another
Please accept the cause was you
You forgot to tie your shoe
So, don't seek to try to sue

For each cause there is effects
Mistakes are not defects
For each and every action
Will have its own reaction
It's the law of attraction

DIFFERENCES

Barbie loves to play with her dolls
Jamie prefers to walk the malls
And Cathy likes to watch the trains
While Pam chooses to brush the manes

It matters not the girl it seems
They all will have much different dreams
One will favor ribbons and bows
Another fancies it. when it snows

I do find. each of them quite dear
With Pam. I play the pioneer
Cathy and I will ride the trains
With dolls we will play when it rains

For none of us are quite the same
Each brings a different claim to fame
All will add something new and grand
And it keeps life from being bland

A YEAR IN ISOLATION

Solitary confinement does much
To make one lose their sense of self
And wonder if they can once again
Communicate with others

Losing the power
Of casual conversation
The ability to open up
Feel comfortable in one's own skin
Becoming fearful when in a crowd

This time can be spent
Delving deep inside
Find the meaning of themselves
Or lose their ability
To think and speak

We are not meant to be
Isolated creatures
A robot at our desks
Never lo look away
From the computer in front of us

It can drive one mad
Losing one's mind
Or make a recluse
Out of someone
Who otherwise was kind

Fearful of acceptance
Tentative and timid
When before they were
Accepting of others
Alas it happens all too often

In today's corporate world
To blame the victim

IF ANIMALS COULD TALK

If animals did talk
What would they say to us
Would they tell us their dreams?
And their clan history
Or the loss of their space
Their fear of all humans

Would humans then adapt
And share in their play
Learn the lessons they have
For the good of all kind
Or put blinders again
Over their eyes and ears

With no wish to know
Continue destruction
And continue to kill
With wanton abandon
For the greed in our hearts
The darkness in our souls

Forgetting once again
The joy we could regain
From the long-lost Eden
And the life we could live
With beauty abounding
Seeking knowledge from all

FOR MY MOTHER

(I understand now.)

Don't take my picture for I fear
You will see that age is creeping up on me
My waistline no longer as slim as once it was
Nor my jawline quite as taut.
The lines of laughter and sorrow have left their mark
And I am searching for me.
Life hasn't been so kind of late
Yet I am still me, you see
Somewhere inside lies the truth
Of who I will be.
For I grow, I learn
I become comfortable again with who I am
And who I am yet to be.
When the ravages of illness have finished with me
And I am free at last
To shed this skin of life
Move on
Into the sun of a new day.

FOR ALL THE JOY

For all the joy you give
The treasured friendship
And sense if sisterhood
Understanding of faults
A glimpse of glory
Given each day to so many
With ease and a smile

If it fits is your motto
Accepting life as it comes
Forgiveness of self
You show us the way
Onwards and upwards
You help us all go

Forever to dance
Life's pleasures and pain
Yet defeat is not yours
You surrender to none
But bring a new view
To all that you touch

WITHIN

Seek thee amongst the lilacs
And the swaying ferns
Where the fields of dandelions
Or wildflowers bloom
Amidst the tall pine trees
And rain-forests too
Look far and wide
Then delve deep within
For the beauty of life
Exists when you're whole within

AN AMOEBA

Stories and tales fill my head
Characters and plots running rampant
In the primordial soup in my mind
Who will scream the loudest?
Which tale will be written first?
Why the one that has grown from an amoeba
And flies from my fingers of course
All will be told when full grown
And leap from my head onto paper
Only to be replaced
By the next primitive lot
That will swim in that proverbial dish

GRAY DAYS

Gray days await
The sun to shine
The spirit is moved
By a glimmer of blue

In these dark winter days
When the world is all bleak

We look to the song
Of the blue jay and cardinal
To give us some color
As we wait for the sun.

AN OGRE I BECOME

An ogre I become
When the words are stewing
And the time is not there
To release the beasts

When they must speak
And I am busy
With day to day projects
While the characters play

I must untwine
Put each with its mate
Let me out they shriek
I am ready to fly

Onto paper and off pen
Out of my spirit they come
Each with its fellows
All in their place

Begone from my head
It's getting crowded you know
It's time to finish one
Then another's turn it will be

Rebecca must burn
To make way for rebirth
For the prophecy to come
And the world built anew

AWAKE SWEET TREE

Awake sweet tree
Your love needs the warmth
A new day is dawning
Breath of spring fills the air
You say it's not time
The beasts of winter still cling
You are probably right
For you understand best
That all in its time
And the time is not yet

FINALLY

Sleep will now come
And I'll soar through the skies
Tiptoe on the clouds
And play in the stars

Rebecca will still burn
And Sadie find light
For the prophecy must come
And the stories will come

FULLNESS

The hawk sits and watches
For the morsel of food
Scarce are the critters
All hiding it seems

Soon he will take flight
His nest will be full
Mouths to feed and skies to roam
The critters will creep out
Of their winter lairs
And the beauty of life
Will awake from its sleep.

JOY

A rainbow's beauty
After a summers rain
Is pale in comparison
To the lovely light
That shines from your eyes
When the joyful laugh
Springs from your soul
And hand and hand
We walk the shore
Together. forever
My husband
My love

RISE AGAIN

High above the ground I soar
Wings spread wide I glide
Into the blue sky I climb
Wild and free I catch the wind
Over the hills my spirit sails
Gloriously I dive
Only to rise again

WIND

My heart climbs
With each breath of air that flows through the trees
Each gust of wind rustling the leaves
As it flows and wraps its powerful arms around the
branches
Nature's fury or quiet glory
Breaths life to the land and into me

LIFE

Today I saw a tree
Alone upon the hill
It was guarding the gate
Protecting the small sapling beside it
One day to take over
When it had grown taller
It's parent now old
The young life will replace
The old one someday
Until then it is sheltered
By its parent so tall
With love for each other
They will weather the storms
With mutual support
Young sapling and old tree

CLOUDS

A road across the sky
It's feathered ladders
For us all to climb
Higher and higher
Up into the stars
Just stretch out your arms
And reach for the moon

DREAMS

Throughout the night I wander
In my dreams I fly
Coasting and gliding
Over hills of green
Meadows where the cattle lo
Horses graze and eagles fly
And wildflowers bloom

Through dark forests
With trees so tall
Creatures fierce and wild
The gentle doe and her fawn
And all manner of life
Large and small
To feast my eyes upon.

Then to crowded cities I might go
To see how others live
Step into someone else's shoes
To experience their thoughts and joys
The heartaches and fears they do not show
I'll see as I live inside them
Understanding better, what I didn't know

And then in the waking world
My heart and soul will carry more
Of life and all its wonder
And compassion will grow

Each night I wander in my dreams
With wonder in my heart
And love for all life's creatures.

Somethings I'll never know
Nor understand completely
But when it is all said and done
I'll not be filled with pain nor hate
Instead my spirit flies with joy
My soul with light and love
Even for that I do not know.

I SHOULD BE

I should be writing or riding
Dancing or cleaning
I should be doing something
That is creative and fun
Or witty and wise
Alas, I can't figure out
Which one. So I'm relaxing.

SPIRIT FILL ME

My heart rises with each breath of air
Every drop of mist fills my soul
I spread my arms to fly with the eagle
Soar the skies, skim the ocean floor
Upon my steed I race over the ground
Wind in my hair, sun on my face
Glorious life fills my spirit
Lifting me higher with wonder and love

A HUNDRED YEARS FROM NOW

One hundred years from now
When this body I now live in
Has become dust again
My energy and thoughts dispersed across the universe
And my spirit a part of the wind
That sweeps the plains and arid lands
Walks with the Yeti, runs with the wolves
Dances upon the rainbows and skips from star to star
My name forgotten even by me
Still I will live, love, and glory in what is.

BEAUTY

Beauty is not in the smoothness of the skin of our youth
Nor the length of our hair. or a wrinkle-free neck
It is not in the shape of breasts or the size of the waist

It is in the way your eyes dance
Your body sways with the music
And the rhythms of life that you live through

It is in the glory that is found in the sunrise
The joy that is yours at sunset
And the heart that reaches for the stars at night

Beauty is in the love and laughter you share
The sorrow and heartache thrown off. from loss and pain
And your ability to see for the best in others

For you are still able to give. feel. and love
And your feet can dance with the wind
Your voice sings with the rain

Arms reach for life and your heart for love
Your spirit able to soar with the birds
And laugh at the antics of the little ones

For in us lies the grace of our youth
The beauty of wisdom. the joy of today
And the hopes and dreams of our tomorrow

REBIRTH

A turkey hawk flew overhead
Followed by a red-tailed hawk
Both beautiful in their magic flight
As they sailed across the sky
A deer peeked out from behind the trees
All barren still
No leaves upon their branches
Although Spring is here
Winters cold hasn't left us yet
Still the magic waits to happen

FROM A DISTANCE

With so much beauty in the world
Sadness and heartache, you cannot change
And only love and hope to Shed sunlight in the dark of night
Why is there so much hate?

What darkness of soul
Must exist to hold onto anger
And attempt to crush
Someone you used to call friend
When they bother you not!

But instead honor your wishes
And leave you alone
Making no waves
Telling no stories
Just wishing you well from a distance

INTO THE WOODS

Into the woods I go
Amongst the tall maples
And full pine trees
I listen for the hawk's wings
The owl's night calls
The movement of the quiet deer
I feel of the wind in my hair
And the silence grows
Within my soul
Filling me with the love and life

I WILL LIVE ON

One thousand years from now
When my body has long since turned to dust
And time has erased my name
Even from my gravestone

My words no longer remembered
Not even by a few
Still I will live on

In the spirit of the wind
In dawn's rising sun
In the first flakes of snow
A kitten's purr or a lion's roar

You will find me.
For I do not measure success
By the money I have made
Nor the lack thereof

But in a heart free from hate
A soul without revenge
The love I hold deep within
Not so tightly that it cannot be seen
But richly, openly, for all that is life.

A WAY INTO LIGHT

The path through loss can be a lonely one
A road that leads to growth
To healing and into magic
Past the tall pines
The long branches swinging in the breeze
Shading and hiding the way
Still the walk should be done
The way must be found
Into the light and out of the dark places.

FOREVER

In the cool breezes of the air
Thoughts of you sweep over me
The sun and moon shine through your eyes
And the gentleness of the softly flowing clouds
Wrap around me
With loving arms of wispy tendrils
Evermore they charm and delight
And in the dark space of my soul
They bring light
Forever and a day

WE WAIT

During the dark and gloomy times
Sometimes all we can do is sniff the air
Listen to the birds
And wait
Wait for the sun to shine
The moon to rise
The stars to once again fill the sky
Wait calmly, clearly, joyfully
Knowing one day
The waiting will end

THE WOLF

Across the fields I race
Through the trees I dart
Over the hills I flee
From the humans
Who hunt
Yet know not what they do

We both mate with our loves
Have families and care
I weep for my lost ones
For the home you destroy
I hunt only to live
And feed those I love

Why do you kill my mate?
And the young of our pack
We could be friends
We have much in common
But some are blind
These humans who kill

PETER

Peter stopped eating
He's eighteen this year
He is our baby
Our playful, loving, orange boy
You loved him like I do

If it's his time to go
Don't let him suffer
Come get him instead
I'll never be ready
But feel blessed with my time

Carry him home
Our sweet orange cat
The last of our furred children
Someday it will be my turn
And when that time comes

I pray that I'll find you both
Happy and healthy again
Don't let him suffer
For I fear it's his time
If not today it won't be long now

Don't let h suffer
If his times at the end
Come get him dear mother
I remember his joy and ours too
The day he became our boy

I remember the years
Of happiness and sorrow
The times that were ours
I'll never forget. I'll never stop loving
The storm is coming in

ACROSS THE YEARS

Across the years my mind flies
Remembering
City streets and bright lights
Dancing till dawn
Buildings that scraped the sky

The memories
Of loves that are long gone
I don't forget
The feelings are still there
Just different

Were we to meet today
Would we still love
My life's so different now
Yesterday's gone

You were a city boy
When our lives touched
Now. I'm a country girl
Seldom in heels
Or the skirts you adored

Instead it's jeans
And long walks in the woods
Or on horseback
Yet the memories last
Dear to me still

All the glorious nights
The laughter shared
And the joy that was then
Yesterday's gone

Happiness is still mine
Just different now

LET GO

Let go. let go. let go
Of all the hurt and pain
The times you wish were different
And those you weren't yourself
The angst you felt
For those you lost
Either through death
Or actions you cannot change
Those clumsy attempts you made
When uncomfortable or sick
Let go. let go. let go
Forgive yourself your follies
For you can't go back and change
But move forward into a lighter place
With peace in your heart and soul
Let go. let go. let go

THE BEST OF ME

I give the best of me
When and what I am able
It is not always what another wants
Sometimes, because I have read it wrong
Occasionally because they don't know themselves
Yet, I know I try to do no harm
At times it appears I fall short
Though not through malice
Nor lack of care.

STORMS

The storm is rolling in
Bringing drenching rain
Ice, sleet, and finally snow
Even the skies mourn
The loss of you.

MOTHER

Today is anniversary
Of your birth
I wish you were here
Even eleven years later
I miss you. my mother. my friend.

MY LOVE

My hips sway
My feet move
My hands flow
My body dances
Music fills my soul
Your voice my ears
Your arms hold me
Not tightly to stop my flight
But strongly to catch me
Should I stumble
You are there
My love
My husband

SAD TO LOSE A FRIEND

I'm always sad to lose a friend
Perhaps we outgrew each other
Maybe a misinterpretation
Whatever it was
It leaves me sorrowful
Just a footprint upon my heart

INFINITY

In a circle of infinity
The Hummingbird holds itself in the air
Wings circling in a figure eight
Beautiful little bird
Shows curiosity for the now
As it glides in and out of the past and future

HAVE YOU NO CONSCIENCE?

Is it that you are born without conscience?
Or was it learned from society
You who put greed above the earth
Take joy in destruction
Pit one against the other
For your war machine

To fill your prisons
Where the poor can work
And die in the name of profit
Destruction is your first name
Greed your middle name
And Hate your last name

For to seek destruction. greed and profit
As your God. with no man or woman
Worthy of your time
Your name can only be
Destruction
Greed
Hate
I have no time for you
Except to wish you'd be
Visited by true conscience
With eyes opened and heart exposed
For you seek death of all that is
In the name of power. greed and profit

SQUISH

I love the mud between my toes
The way it squishes and the way it flows
And when I walk it splashes high
Over my heels and onto my thighs
Splotches cover me from head to toe
It's soft and cool and better than snow

Helen Diessner

YOU'RE GONE

You laughed, and I couldn't help but smile and wonder what
marvelous story I had just missed.
The sound of your laughter, seemed to travel through my
entire being,
And rest deep in my mind, staying with me long after
You were gone.
The often cold and stern demeanor you displayed was so
misunderstood, even by me.
I would be happy to see your aloof countenance once more,
but
You're gone
Buried deep inside you was this kind and gentle soul that I
was honored to experience.
I saw you cry for all the pain that was buried in your past.
Pain you were afraid to share, lest it crush your tender
heart further.
If only I could once again hold and comfort you, but
You're gone.
The wonderful day trips we made, laughing and sharing
nature made me smile.
For me it's impossible to get behind the wheel of my car
without recollecting these times,
Yearning once more for these shared adventures.
But you're gone.
In silence I wept for you when you became ill, not wanting
you to know
Because, you would then weep for me

I had to leave you, and it almost broke my heart each time I
went to see you.
I was afraid to hold you because you were so thin and sick.
My selfishness wants to do these days over
But you're gone.
My heart wants to believe that you're still here.
My mind knows that we'll meet again.
But for now, you're gone.

Helen Diessner

MAYBE WHEN

When the old are dying in the street
Your sons are off at war
Your daughters pregnant yet again
With another they cannot feed.
Maybe then....

When the soil is tainted
With ash and soot
Chemicals beyond repair
And food cannot be grown
Maybe then...

When the air is unbreathable
For small or large
Creatures dying from lack of air
And the dead are lying in the streets
Maybe then...

When the water can no longer hold
Fish or foal
So, polluted by mankind's waste
And not even from a bottle can it be drunk
Maybe then...

When the money is gone
For a debt called in
That cannot be repaid
And the government is laid to waste
Maybe then...

When the press can only report
What the big man says
How bigly we are
And how wonderful the war is going
Maybe then...

When the bombs start flying
Destruction is everywhere
Children lying in blood upon the ground.
And life is nearly gone
Maybe then...

We'll learn he should have kept
His hands away from tweets
Nor should he have sold us out
After our country is gone.
Maybe then...

We'll know it wasn't about our race
The color of our skin
The way we practiced our faith
Nor the language we spoke.
Maybe then...

Roman Nyle

The emotions and thoughts that go into poetry can be beautiful, painful and powerful. They are individual to the poet and often extremely personal, telling more about the individual than any other type of book.

Thank you, Helen Diessner, and Roman Nyle for allowing us to put one of your poems into this book.

Marta Moran Bishop
www.martamoranbishop.com

Crowe Press
www.crowepress.com

www.ingramcontent.com/pod-product-compliance
Lightning Source LLC
Chambersburg PA
CBHW070048040426
42331CB00034B/2631